W9-BZE-619

COCHISE

By the same author

Collections
THE AFTERNOON IN DISMAY
FAT MAN POEMS
TERMS AND RENEWALS
WILD'S MAGICAL BOOK OF CRANIAL EFFUSIONS
PELIGROS
NEW AND SELECTED POEMS

Chapbooks
THE GOOD FOX
MICA MOUNTAIN POEMS
SONNETS
MAD NIGHT WITH SUNFLOWERS
LOVE POEMS
DILEMMA: BEING AN ACCOUNT OF THE WIND THAT
BLOWS THE SHIP OF THE TONGUE
GRACE

COCHISE

Peter Wild

Doubleday & Company, Inc.
Garden City, New York
1973

UNIVERSITY OF TOLEDO LIBRARIES

ISBN: 0-385-03876-3 Trade
0-385-05792-X Paperbound
Library of Congress Catalog Card Number 73-79725
Copyright © 1969, 1972, 1973 by Peter Wild
All Rights Reserved
Printed in the United States of America
First Edition

Many of the poems in this book were first published in periodicals: THE
BUFFALO, POEM, *Poetry*, Copyright © 1972 Modern Poetry Associa-
tion; RÍO PUERCO, *Road Apple Review*, Copyright © 1972 by RAR;
POLLEN, *Chicago Review*, Copyright © 1972 by Chicago Review,
EVENT IN ROME, *University of Wisconsin Review*, Copyright © 1973
by Wisconsin Review; ORACLE FROM RED RIDGE, NORA, *University
of Wisconsin Review*, Copyright © 1971 by Wisconsin Review; A TRAV-
ELLER SITTING BENEATH A MIMOSA TREE LOOKING OUT AT
AN ANCIENT LANDSCAPE, *Rain*, Copyright © 1971 by Rain;
SAILORS, *Bachy*, Copyright © 1972 by Papa Bach Bookstore; PIC-
TURE OF TWO COWBOYS TALKING, *Salt Lick*, Copyright © 1971 by
Salt Lick Press; A TIGHT FIX, MANTEQUILLA DE CACAHUATE,
Charas, Copyright © 1971, 1972 by Claire Levenhagen, respectively;
NEW HOME, THOMAS AND CHARLIE, *The Far Point*, Copyright ©
1972 by The University of Manitoba Press; THE HOBO, *Lillabulero;* SUN-
DAY, *The Falcon*, Copyright © 1972 by Mansfield State College; ODE
TO GASTON SANTOS, THE FABULOUS BULLFIGHTER ON HORSE-
BACK, *The Carleton Miscellany;* HARV, *Ark River Review*, Copyright
© 1972 by The Ark River Review; RIDING DOUBLE, *Antaeus;* THE
ABSTRACTIONIST, *Foxfire*, Copyright © 1972 by Southern Highlands
Literary Fund, Inc.; TAKING A WALK WITH THE DOG, *Motive*,
Copyright © 1970 by Board of Education of the United Methodist
Church; THE CANDIDATE, *Poetry Northwest*, Copyright © 1971 by
The University of Washington; THE WEREWOLF, *Amython*, Copyright
© 1972 by Amython; SANTA TERESAS, *Ironwood*, Copyright © 1972
by Ironwood Press; THE BURNING GIRAFFE, *TransPacific*, Copyright
© 1971 by Nicholas Crome; THE COWBOY, THE FAT LADY, *Uni-
versity of Windsor Review;* SINS OF THE TONGUE, *Puerto Del Sol*,
Copyright © 1972 by Puerto Del Sol; SALVATION, *Minnesota Review*,
Copyright © 1972 by New Rivers Press; THE NIGHT-BLOOMING
CEREUS, *Inscape*, Copyright © 1972 by the Baleen Press; SUN TEA,
Greenfield Review, Copyright © 1972 by the Greenfield Review.

Several of the poems were reprinted in a small chapbook, GRACE,
published by The Stone Press.

PS
3573
.I42C6

Para mi esposa,
Otra vez

Contents

Reveille   I

The Seduction   3
Sawtooths   5
Río Puerco   7
Pollen   9
The Buffalo   11
The Cobbler   13
Pilots   15
Event in Rome   17
A Traveller Sitting Beneath a Mimosa Tree
     Looking Out at an Ancient Landscape   19
Sailors   21
Picture of Two Cowboys Talking   23
A Tight Fix   25
Flight from Cortez   27
Pulling Weeds   29
New Home   31
The Indians   33
Tamarisk   35
The Hobo   37

Cochise   II

Sunday	41
Ode to Gaston Santos,	
the Fabulous Bullfighter on Horseback	43
Harv	45
Owl Heads	47
The Extraction	49
Oracle from Red Ridge	51
Nora	53
Riding Double	55
The Abstractionist	57
Taking a Walk with the Dog	59
The Horse	61
Climbers	63
The Observers	65
The Candidate	67
Thomas and Charlie	69
The Werewolf	71
Santa Teresas	73

The Burning Giraffe   III

The Burning Giraffe	77
The Cowboy	79
Sins of the Tongue	81
Poem	83
The Farmer from Iowa	85
Mantequilla de Cacahuate	87
The Poor	89
The Harp and the Goat	91
The Fat Lady	93
Cochise	95
Dog Hospital	97

Salvation   99
Juan Sin Miedo   101
The Night-Blooming Cereus   103
Phelps-Dodge   105
Sun Tea   107

Reveille   I

The Seduction

You cross thousands of miles of desert
        arriving with a broken axle
   and one leg half torn off;
wander through our groves
        all day drinking water, water.

we send you out
     to toughen you up
   through children lining the streets,
      who band around you
  waving their flags, waving their underwear
waiting to hear you say just one dirty word.

from our porch at sunset
      see you well under way,
head down still crawling
        in the right direction,
     dragging one leg.

and months later hear from an old trader
     what we already knew
   that you found an Indian girl
    with turquoise hair,
   built her a lodge;
  that every evening she stoops over
      your bare heaving chest,
   with both hands
     feasts on your heart,
and every morning with a kiss,
     like a puff of air across your forehead
    wakes you up.

Sawtooths

There will be a farmer standing
among clods
arms the vines
of his own old squashes
reaching down, reaching up.
his face bleached venison
stops to listen.
while miles away his wife
who uses dung for snuff
runs around the frame house
that the light has begun to eat
crossing herself. a
cornice falls off, shouting
slogans of salvation from every
window. and away at Friendly Corners
the buttocks of retired wrestlers
absorb the bar stools, they watch the
plastic pistols wink glued to the bark.
up there beyond the nails of crags
smoking meadows, pools
Indians open their eyes, put on
feather gowns, begin to
march around, as the clouds
roll over the rock, curl, take fire,
to chase the golden mountain lions
that circle, circle. new rivers
pour out of the sky. where the
Colonel had a wash dug across
three counties with rusting machines he sees
a Spanish battalion rise out of the ground—sunk
in mud a hay rake opens its mouth—fresh,
plumes floating, armor newly pumiced.
jaws charcoal, singing, they march
toward him, through him toward the mountains,

where a roar begins in the very tendrils
of his scrotum. the huge saw blades
shudder, begin to move.
they scratch back and forth
across her heart
across his heart.

Río Puerco

Across the sky
the women have spread their dirty blankets,
where the last crow flies,
a tuft of arrows splitting from a rainbow

out in the river the mud
begins to bubble, rising
in a tent, a head with globes of water
for eyes that look around

your pistols have fallen to your knees.
you look through the holes in your stomach
and the body below torn from its skin
is red fiber and dried sinew

which is why you clutch the santo
to your breasts, one side an idiot
and the other, standing in lilies
the image of yourself

which is why you fall on the stones to sleep,
the corners of bread eat at your stomach
and all night the trees groan above you
like a woman giving birth.

Pollen

The armies have awakened
before reveille. they lie on their backs
in the phlegmy dawn.
what has brought them to this? they
pick up their wet tools.
when the sun comes up they pin
on their delicate wings and
spread out. the enemy is sleeping just over the hill
like a sotted cow. they
know they will win.

The Buffalo

The buffalo come to the place drunken from sleep
and drink at the pool, lowering their eyes
at the new water that floods over the grass,
shying at the clouds that ripple toward them
and burn around their ankles like a liquid fire.

back in their heads toy carts
begin spinning their wheels. soldiers
emerge shining from mud eating chocolate
from flowers of tin foil, and girls, breasts
bound high in perfumed nets mount them
waving their ribbons and hats.

it stings them like a cool iron bee slipping
off the clouds, a spear piercing the hide
and making their tongues move the
air into new words. the Indians are gathering
in the earth, the ground moves, and the mountains
bristle in new places.

they come murmuring and smelling like them
flashing shields before their snouts that show them their faces,
feather trains making snakes in the wind around them.
they fade, they buck, they rear
their white shoulders high into the moonlight

and their small hooves cut the earth
as they dodge following their mocking steps.
the crude stone axes chop into the humps
and hack at the gristly ball in the hip.
where the clouds were steel holes appear,
they feel their tiny organs drawn into air.

The Cobbler

At night you will hear strange noises.
your wife will say it is your drinking
but convinced, starting down the stairs
                                with your gun
below the darkness is full of voices,
                like burning straw
        like charred bones singing in the wind.

those are your good deeds.
and turning, afraid,
                you start back up
as they reach for your nightshirt,
                reach for your hair,
        rising in the space toward you
                        climbing over each other
on arms and elbows
                thin and fragile as spaghetti.

in the morning everything is the same.
                you sit on the wooden edge of the bed
        and shrug at the stare,
sit before your bench
                arms buoyed with coffee
        as she knocks about upstairs with the broom
and the pieces fly through your hands
                taking their shapes

as you remember they always did.
                and on holidays out walking
        at last alone, see them
                        like your children
white as udders
                hanging in the trees,
        off in the fields dancing along
                a cow's back.

13

and later along the fence,
   tired, a stone in wet moss
   that opens into a heart
      with teeth in it
trying to mouth vowels,
    that beckons for your hand.
you stoop, draw back
   and take the long way home
to the days filled with sunlight,
      the sleepless quaking nights.

Pilots

The fire has halted
at the end of the pier
where the blind stand
holding up their sores.
after dropping from the sky
in the uniform of a pilot,
burning the vegetable stalls, the museums,
running through the streets
on its own oil like a tongue
they stand enraged, rags and filth
falling from their arms
as it spits and sucks.
behind them out at sea unawares the sky
opens in one white line
like a purplish boxer's eye.
Indians charge out bent over their buffalo.
they turn and see their names
floating in toward the piles, folding on the waves.
and before them in the flames those men
those sad saints looking much like them
who edge closer, shuffling, beckon. . . .

Event in Rome

You come running out of the temple
a sky growing in your mouth,
landscape of ancient pastures,
lions and amphoras in the distance.
in the foreground a few eyes move in the trees,
sequins that sparkle with small engravings of heroes.

the bullets fall from around your waist.
you are out on the marble now
that lies back in a crystalline dust.
swinging around the belly button
that is a target, a spiral folding
through you, a long tail
sucking in the scent of your flesh.
you smile as for a picture. but
figures are moving in the stone all around
you, sharks and bloated swimmers
fighting toward the surface for a long breath.

on the train you begin screaming
that this is an operating table
that the chairs are surgical instruments.
that the sickly light is eating you
and will go out. I pull your head
into the window by your braids
and use your halter to tie you to the seat.
you want to rape yourself.
your breasts are fried eggs that
sink into your chest as you stare ahead.

A Traveller Sitting Beneath a
Mimosa Tree Looking Out at an Ancient Landscape

He's a long way
from where he's come,
a land where they speak no language,
people all red
and the savages file their teeth,
twist their women black into knots.
no matter:
turbaned he needs no money,
carries the ancient, stable
documents in his sleeves.
across the way faces pass
through the sandstone cliffs
slow as a storm coming,
at times lightning through heat,
spines drawn through the flesh.
no man speaks;
there are no women.
and that is as it should be,
and on the occasion it
is with the tried dictums.
a thorn bush starved for centuries
at his elbow, living.
he leans on his staff
keeping the clouds
from going fuzzy,
from passing through his head.
to have no sin,
no history
worth remembering;
at night after one
pipe of it he sleeps
in the rocks, rigid,
porcelain fingers, porcelain chin.

Sailors

If he smokes too much
the insides of his mouth
      become the walls of a cave
spreading with moss agate.
his molars rise from the gums
    like sailors miraculously pushed out
  of the waves which have almost drowned them.
yet salvation is painful;
      they are not yet saved.
and they must tumble wide-eyed
  losing their belts, their rope soles
in the stream of blood, a bubbling hand
    curving down from his tongue,
      calling for their mothers;
the birds snatch them from the flood
  like crumbs,
      bear them off lamenting
    the cathedrals of his nostrils
  to the desert islands.

Picture of Two Cowboys Talking

After all those years
the eyes grow thin
with the light, until they
are two luminous strips
pasted on the cloud of the head,
                              remembering
nothing but what the bones
tell them.
and the hands crack
as boots crack;
the oyster rattles
around in its leather shell.
years drinking from tinajas,
                    something to the bowels—
a way to sleep,
growing into it like a tree.
hard nights in town.

they sit in the back yard,
negatives against the sun, wreathed,
beneath real trees
talking, and then go in,
but not as boys do
in the night at times,
get out the guns,
slip cartridges in and out,
work the actions. . . .

A Tight Fix

Claw-quick the cloak
wrapped about his arm,
a shield leaping from the snow
the bolt of his knife and knees, a dream
dripping all his hearts, and maze
of gold chain flourished before
the bear's face, who like a tree
from the rain rears back, but with
claws raised, bloody tentacles from the mouth,
and a jet-black skull, and waits
to teeter on the boy—behind every oak
his friends can do nothing but shoot
and shoot, through them both, faster than
they dreamed with ease, until the creature dives
at the boy's feet, goes on sailing down
down. . . . fallen to the snow
the youth watches him go, with no scream,
spread-eagle, a puppet going to no hell,
kneeling, bewildered, rocked by shock
on shock of lightning. . . .

Flight from Cortez

At night airplanes take off
on mysterious missions
behind them the watery lights
    on the desert airports go off
like flowers closing up in the dark.
past Naahtee, past Twin Buttes, Totacon,
hearing them go over, big cigars, ribbed insects
       over the midnight ruins, over the cold cedars,
the Indians look up and their eyes tear
back in long yellow tears
to their ears. their feet grow claws
and paw at the snow like men on bicycles.
they tear at their blankets with their teeth
       and pull out thin strings.
their sheep lie dead all around them.
    while a few lambs sleeping
tumble after in the wash, fall
or rise becoming green stars.
when they arrive it is like a groom
   smiling, arriving at a surprise party.
all the lights of the city come on.
crowds of high-school girls are there
      throwing flowers,
they crank down the mountains,
and two strong men carry out the
    stewardess
whose teeth have replaced her words,
whose breasts have replaced the air,
strap her into a chair. she is
hysterical or drunk on what the future
will bring. and laughing her fingers
white spiders over her face take off. . . .
the lights go down, the mountains come up again. . . .

Pulling Weeds

My hands grow stiff from the slaughter
a man killing snakes and pigs.
in knee-pants I wade through the yellow flood
              filling the yard, not clinging
but like ink slipping,
             angel faces, bodies twisting

already sunflowers shut their eyes,
      freeze against the gore on their cheeks,
and the clouds float in through the trees,
          tainted, to lick and feed.

kites are up in the neighborhood, venomous girls
             undressing to paper.
brows going sharp, legs chewed
    I climb up the gangplank of the sidewalk
into the bowels of the house
        and wait.
        sweat dries tattoos
           of my cooling sins over me.
my hand falls through the puddle of my chest;
three tall kings walk through the street,
                   rolled snow and weeds,
     bowing, waving their arms slowly,
        humming through their bark teeth.

New Home

It takes us years to find it,
driving all night up and down Speedway,
following the roads at the ends of roads
until going back we see Dick's light, in his gym suit
standing a star in the blossoming creosote.
and he gets in after all these years telling us
about the mad ranch woman
who built these houses, directing each stone
into the terraces, the patios, and a reservoir
with its whispering rat sounds as you walk beneath each floor.
the little car can hardly make it over the lip
of the hill, around the cactus and shattered boulders,
then we see a tower
the bastion, crenels, teeth spread on the ground.
we spend the rest of the night feeling our way around the house,
climbing through windows into sunken rooms,
admiring the fireplace big enough for a man roast—
you say only crazy people have lived here,
and at night sometimes the coyotes
come up and stare in your windows.
finally we stand beneath a few stars
        in the sound only of the moon letting
down its net over the lumped charcoal desert.

The Indians

The trumpets blow
and Columbus stands on his island
the blue back of a tortoise
waving his reed sword
inviting the Indians to come ashore.
they advance stooped over, smiling,
bacon dripping from their lips, turning more red.
he lets them examine him, plunging
their hands through the holes, offers
them a model of the ship they came in.
they offer him baubles which he
inspects to be polite, then puts aside.
he notices the island is small and sinking
but invites them into his tent, the
size of an envelope. inside the hall
is paved with Bibles; they smoke
and call the terms back and forth.
finally the warriors outside rush in and bear him off
on their shoulders like a wooden corpse.
not used to such speed he watches the
clouds above and asks an assistant
for the latest messages from the king. at
camp they marry him off to their
most intelligent princess, let
him keep his notebooks and pistols. he spends
the rest of his life growing a moustache,
drunk in a blanket, squints at his children
running off over the hills like red
ants to conquer the world.

Tamarisk

Adobes begin appearing through the neighbor's
old wall as the lone tamarisk tree even now
being struck by lightning holds out
the new stubs of its hands while
growing sleek shoots from the elbows.
snow blows into the stucco corners of his porch;
long ago the geese have betrayed him
running away from the swampy place in his yard,
risking the desert to find another morning
and the sun rising on a soft creamy ocean.
he sits inside buried in his coat as
his legs become burnished by the fire, more like wood
remembering the revolution and his cold youth on the campo
while I have just moved here. sometimes
the snowclouds sweep down off the mountains
and sailors in their pea coats appear in the rutted streets
red-faced, calling to each other, trying our back doors
while cold-fingered we wait inside, listening
            to the heat rattle up our chimneys.

The Hobo

They don't know where you've been, or
where you're going.
but only that you are
for the moment, a fact, an un-
pleasant assertion. stick around.

Cochise II

Sunday

When you come over
the sparrows are nesting in the eaves
rattling among the dead vines

as we sit
straight in the antique chairs
the house going quiet
they spurt, flak across the evening
or floating, the tail of a kite,
the black hair of an angel
                              treading
against the clear winter sky.

we sit so still
it settles around us,
sinking to the sills.
you drop your head
take another sip from the can
and tell me about your boss
who communicates by long letters
you find on your desk in the mornings, how
he is in good with the vice-president—
you move to go pick up your daughter
          from the birthday party

but we sit awhile
like those birds you read about
that live entirely at sea
and never sleep,
floating at night on the water, wide-awake
with the moon and the debris.

Ode to Gaston Santos, the Fabulous
Bullfighter on Horseback

You are a babyfaced boy
        on a Nogales poster,
unusually blonde
    and slightly apprehensive,
like a recent college graduate;

and when you ride your horse
                trapped in flowers
through the topsy-turvy streets,
    the tattered girls throw roses,
swoon,
        showing black teeth
                through their taut lips,
dreaming of you in red coat and blonde hair
        clutched forever in their arms.

and you sail up
        over the rooftops in shambles
soar over the bull ring,
        your horse pawing the clouds
like in a slow-motion film,
smiling down at us magnificently
        from a great distance. . . .

I'm sure, though,
        after you have swabbed your cracked
lips with vinegar
                and run to your moment in the circle,
    that you prick the bull real good
            right down to his aorta,
without pretense,
            and the muscles
of your forearm bulge
            athletically.

43

oh, I'm sure you sleep as I do,
        babyfaced, and with a pistol
by your bed,
        both arms enfolding
your foam-rubber pillow,
                and dreaming
of white-fleshed women,
        pumping big-haunched as they ride,
grassy hair streaming behind them,
                across your hard world.

Harv

We are happy to hear you are moving to Australia
after years in the ghetto
living on nothing, getting out
with a good job and a degree. glad when your wife
giggles on the telephone, and says your father-in-law, doctor
of the old school, has divorced
and married a twenty-two-year-old girl who's pregnant.
you let your kid talk whose head
I almost crushed swinging the baby
up past the rafter in the apartment—
he says   Hello   How are you   Good-bye.
perhaps you'll swing by this summer.
and what will we do?—trade
wives on the tiny-gravelled roof beneath
a full moon while the children sleep
curled in the gauze tent like worms. I
remember when Liz was away visiting for a rest,
one Saturday night you ended the party
at 3 a.m. in your Superman suit
standing flexed on the sofa, whistling, hands out,
and dove, the homemade cape
following behind as you did a perfect double
roll, landing on the rug like a
Moslem praying, and went to sleep.

Owl Heads

All day
driving south from Phoenix
down the alluvial plain
that the mountains scattered
on both sides gave us
old teeth
around a tongue
still growing,
in their sunlight
running away.
past the lushness
of cactus
standing in the snow
going everywhere beyond us
that they might be
gravestones
of jeweled instruments
curiously singing in the cold.

for hours past weaving trailers
moving homes
that make my hands shake
and on the freeway over towns
one garage open,
the lips of houses buttoned
pitching slowly into the ground.

in just the right light
slanting over the mountains
you can make them out
far off the highway,
heads twitching this way and that,
or one, a beak sunken in its breast,

surprised at the light, at whatever we've found
as a farmer plows.
though we hesitated
climbing them once
was nothing,
sat in a big eye a cove
from the wind,
and on the bald top
scrambling up
nails, some surveyor's junk.

now they slip behind us
mouths open,
chains of pale-turquoise
seeds around their foreheads,
toes in mud.
and we get off the freeway just
as the lights are coming on around the city.
in the living room our flesh
still hums from the driving.
go through all the cupboards
for something to eat.

The Extraction

When you come in
you are a rubber raincoat
covered with blood
when I kiss you where
your lips were
when I kiss your hands red
as a saint's hands
and hug you you collapse
and I see the doll's legs hanging out.

it is true what the philosophers
say about moonsheep
that they are spores full of light
the dangerous mushrooms give off.
they have slipped from the inert
bodies of violas and stand
among the rocky meadows smiling
like girls who can never go home.

just before you slip back into yourself
a cigarette paper falls from your mouth
with the shipping lanes of the world
pencilled on it. I see the underside
of your tongue, and your eyes spin
round like revolving doors, like
the eyes of sailors who stay drunk ashore
cursing us, then reel back to drown in their own water.

Oracle from Red Ridge

Below us Oracle sleeps,
a stone thrown up from an ancient prophet's
lips that he had chipping the enamel,
working against the muscle.
mornings a spattered piece of green saliva
star-shaped that slips with the hours
toward a lion in the noon, head split at the edge
of the bare foothills that haven't moved
yet, not caring
that under the folds he keeps crossed eyes.
below us, thousands of feet, the Mormons
wear out the bottoms of their pants, spit
and nod toward the tourists.
while up here we know the birds
can fly through our heads, we have heard
the crows calling us in syllables of our flesh.
around our knees
the ferns have a possibility of wings.
we get up to go and one hand against a tree
you feel faint, pitch into the needles
and dribble at the lips. while hours
later when the sun has passed through your face
changing it again, we have
made it out, your gear piled on my gear,
light as an angel dancing at the end of my hand.
stand in the ridge pines as the wind and shadows
give back your color. and before plunging
down to the car see how it must look
tonight, a coal floating across the black desert. . . .

Nora

All summer
you will sit watching
            the ribs of the corral,
across the highway the grasslands
beneath a constant sun turning silver filament
south to the black penline of mountains.

sit in its stench looking at the Beef Cafe
shrinking into its wood
where the tourists won't visit,
hung with old chiles over curling paint.
you will be afraid to go down the one street
barefoot to the closed school,
past the neighbors' fences,
out to the spring where you and Tony Ramirez
used to ride all day and picnic.
the afternoon growing frosts of nails
                    that tear the skin and
paper birds that slice across the eye.

mornings you will wake as if born anew
                            into water,
the Virgin emerging from the pink-plastered adobe;
your mother in the kitchen, alone,
            cooking a little breakfast for you both;
you will slip on your shorts.

but things move under your hands like animals,
the sun making shadows on the land.

a blade grows into your chest
splitting the sternum, that you taste
when you eat;
clouds pass through your breasts,
                    through the slots of your eyes.

at night when you peel off your bra
you take off your womanhood;
the organs flop out,
tame dogs.

O Virgin wherever you stand,
        on hanging cardboard feet
    above a swamp of tules,
is mud or gold, a book too dull to read.

while a furry boy takes shape in your bowels,
begins to eat up your throat,
licks at your ears
        as birds pass through your hands. . . .

Riding Double

You think they might come
tandem, swinging buckets,
        their fishermen's coats on;
the vines let go, ashes from the screen
            seeking wells, burning roots
        into the hours of the afternoon

one has a mask on
    showing only her eyes
and the teeth sticking out
        parallel to the ground;
she stares at you,
    body a bag of pumping muscle.
behind, all buckskin, he whirls his thunder rod;
    they stand still.

and the trees begin their wheels
                spiked with birds,
        ribbons and a thousand whistles;
these cut across your nose:
        those two going off in a smoke,
    a grinning salad.
and instead of the sun
        an iron ship glides into the deserted horizon.

The Abstractionist

Falling and falling through your webs
feet out stiff, clutching your baby gun,
one among hundreds in baggy suits pegged
looking down in the dark to see your toes
where the Chinks wait in their dugouts
       reading books, playing records,
to rush out clapping and bang their cymbals
aim their plastic straws and shoot
striped candy and mints, a new morning when you land,
moving, an icicle in a snowstorm; you thumb your bolt.
while at home the wife drives daily
a hundred miles back and forth to her mother's,
thinking she's a Cherokee, and hated by your mother,
also ballooning, having another; so what
was there to do crawling out but
paint the clouds, clouds that were really gods
you fell through, smear it on your legs
and throat, whether in the States or Mexico
because changing, in that respect, they
were the same everywhere, bursts or weather; have
it approved for government pay at a school. and next,
knowing better, to wear a necktie
and play the same fool, a hole through the fence.
they came and painted sunsets,
you tried avoiding ladies
and luncheons in the afternoons, community
service. and now, outranked again,
your three daughters romp around the house
climbing the walls, spreading out, them-
selves becoming clouds while women around
grow fat and more talkative,
yourself becoming cumulus. to
have just one good exhibition;

57

                              to sit
chunky in the bank and watch the
smiles, be picked over. drifting,
spreading, until the fingers themselves
become too thin, musing, to wear
paint-stained pants and smelly shirts,
falling backwards through yourself toward
new shapes, the moon on spreading mists,
where here in West Texas, land, clouds, and people,
the parents have heard about such things. . . .

Taking a Walk with the Dog

Things change so fast that
you can hardly count
            on the dictionary anymore;
Laramie for instance, pop. 17,520
        which I'm sure has changed since then
    or Orange County, which in the
                last ten years has skyballed,
space industries springing from the furrows

so that a farmer can hardly be himself.
        and this old house, sold from
    hand to hand, redone; no one
                can remember the
                proper owner.
in Southern California you can't
        go away for a year without
    coming back a stranger:
streets torn up, friends moved,
                new malls and civic centers

these government programs
            the country going crazy growing.
        even the dog loves her old sock
and hunts nervous around the house
            when we have to wash it.
behind our eyes is something
                like Oklahoma,
        a place nobody wants.
or Alpine for instance
            too old and feeble to know better,
    two hundred miles from the nearest airport;
yet even here they have a vague idea
        of progress, pains from lumbago
            built low-rent units for the aged.

we walk to the edge of town,
            to where the prairie starts.
the lights come on behind us.
            a satellite keels over.

The Horse

Whenever the sheets are out
he can be found in his glass house
banging the piano with a taco,
the top of his head pulled back like the visor
of a helmet. smoke pours out of his mouth.
stamps his hooves on the pedals
singing, watching the blue girl
in her bottle flutter, flutter up on the shelf.
over the brush and sand dunes
over the distant litmus mountains
the fusees begin going off behind his cerebellum,
all around in the dry afternoon.
he looks down and he has a crinoline dress on
his maps begin jumping, spreading into the walls;
the music sticks to the end of his nose.
and as she goes faster, as her tail glows, splits,
snow and an ash fill the room,
he rears back, howls; a train
puffs out of the swamp, like a snake,
encircles the house. above
him his beer begins to boil.

Climbers

The further they go
the less they leave behind.
though they start out snorting,
stamping their feet, the wind
like teeth in their ears. spreading out
the meadows burn white, the cows
looming in the trail, red-eyed, ashes
that disintegrate; their straw hats
smoke, their rubber gums blow away. and steeper,
astounded by the mystery of their glass thighs
bulging into their faces, behind their packs
like their lungs ahead floating. and finally
risking everything in those hot, high places,
struggle through sand like water around their waists,
collapse onto the gravel of an old riverbed,
cinders falling into themselves, their staffs
beside them snakes, followed
by that old one-eyed Indian, and the coyote,
a puff of wind limping behind.

The Observers

Across the street the old lady
whose husband spends his nights
keeping track of the stars
is out in her front yard again kneeling,
squinting into her grass.
at intervals she opens her mouth
and between the needles, from her nose
flames shoot out. they make the pebbles hop
the bones of ants fly with the dust and
the grass withers back from her for awhile.
the whole family has travelled to India
to see them sweating through the jungle,
to see them from all directions, scaling
bare mountains in the Argentine or clinging
like starved birds with their telescopes from masts.
and I have heard them at night
in the middle of my sleep
their whispers and giggles as the top
of their house opens, the commands as they point
the oiled machines. . . .
but as she squats now blowing
her son stands out in the green polo field
absentminded, making sliding butterflies with his
rod and a moth on the line—see
her daughter just up the street
up in the trees naked and chased
by all the boys of the neighborhood.
lightning drips from between her ribs
fire from her eyes as she stands braced
then flips and they groan tumbling after.
while in his bloody robes and
pointed hat, behind his hair clotted with gore
he climbs slowly up the tower following
his white hands in front, the spider bones of his fingers,

murderer of white moths and wet flowers.
and I watching her straighten
to fill her lungs, to make another puff
hear my horse out back stomping
on the patio, who has eaten the woodpile
and will greet me cross-eyed
as he chews into the mulberry's trunk.

The Candidate

Mornings he spits out a few
>> rotten teeth with the toothpaste
> and a little green blood.
> gold doubloons roll from his belly.
and with a crust of toast
>> still wedged in his mouth

he begins running through the day
>>> in his rubber suit
> running toward his shadow
a brown smoke
>> he hopes to never jump through,
pursued by other shadows,
>>> with nails
>> and lugged boots

targets popping up, girls
> and corpses lunge from bushes,
tear at his clothes
>> or stand pointing at their exposed
>>>> organs

through the vague afternoon storms
> that circle, curling strips of bacon;
and a cat as big as a house
>> bristling with baskets

finally having feasted
>>> on leather and tendons
> locked in his home,
> folds himself into bed;
> lies a machine in its crate.
the wolf-eared moon
>> steps out of the hedges,
> lays its chin on his sill. . . .

Thomas and Charlie

Here where the parrots come down
                out of the morning fog,
            out of the fog that hangs along the river
    to flash through the bamboo
                    tearing out the night's shoots
            or sit on a cow's back
    and eat raw hamburger from a waiter's hand
you wake having travelled all night through
    the sweat of your friends,
                            the dusty comics
sick farmers by the road
                and the peaks
        jumping out of the clouds into the moon,
to see the buttocks of the fat busdriver where
        he rolled from his hammock drunk
    and slept
    hearing over the hill the morning traffic—
you know where you are
        and breaking the dust from your lids
    breaking your back
climb up the veranda
            still slick and dripping dew
    to be the first one
                to hear the farmers singing

        off in their lost valleys,
        to see again the innkeeper's thirteen
                        mythical daughters
that make you famous,
        tight in Levi's through the smoke of your coffee,
here where the llamas could be gold spindles
    where you could wear a gold ring in your ear,
    and the adventuresome tourist
            taking his black veins in his teeth

drives with his wife locked behind
in the trailer for fear
for weeks through the spiralling mountains,
to reach the top and see
they have slipped away into the mists. . . .

The Werewolf

Circling
I draw you closer
to yourself, my hard-
bellied sheep, so
that you sit in the hogan
pistol pointed at the door,
freezing in your sweat while I walk around walk around
beating my arms, making snarls and gestures
to the stars you can only imagine through the walls,
until you fall through your arms
as any man would, until you wake
and look out hungry, lung-struck by the snow;
see my clean footprints, razors
on the toes, with none leading in
and none leading out; and beyond
the low mountains, which also dig
their claws in, lower their heads
                and begin to crawl. . . .

Santa Teresas

Starting at the bottom
with our provisions
a tin of dull cake, maps
rolled up the leg holes
we spread along the white trail
gouged and blasted from rock
passing the fern-coves,
through sweat tears,
numb in rainbows,
passing through the songs and stubble
the shadows of ourselves
until the whole body strung out
can find no holds
and we move the ghost of a lung
on welted calloused soles
coming out among the dead piñons
where there was no top. below
the planes of the San Pedro
slide back and forth on their colors.
Coronado revels in his history
singing to his sainted bastard children.
and forty miles away the Santa Teresas
stand up, a grey block, an erect clitoris.
we take out our knives and stab our hands
the flesh slides from our bones—
the lions come whirling at us through
the trees like snakes, and then away.

The Burning Giraffe   III

The Burning Giraffe

Where have you found
water
in the rivers of sand
where the dunes fold on fold,
among coves where the sunlight
pools upon itself here and there into shadows,
as along a body.

you look down into the invisible water
with eyes that are ball bearings,
eyes of a woman,
where the white-haired girls twine and untwine,
fading and rising toward you like threads.

while behind on a hillock an Arab
raises his sequined rifle
in the hand
embroidered with shell and bone,
for a warning, a victory,
smoke pouring from his curls,
shows his fig teeth.

and you are gone to your home
among the shadows,
into the swine of the mountains.

when the frost congeals on my skin like a fur,
rising like those having all their teeth pulled
the flower disappears up my nose,
a stone melts into thin air;
and you are still there
somewhere
rising on legs
shaky as roads on a map
going north.

The Cowboy

Everywhere he went he saw
birds shooting out of the cracked earth,

foam rising over a hill
from a distant ocean. he

didn't go for his gun.
the cows still eyed him

and he carried it in his nostrils
and ears, the burning flesh
that later flowered green

and the ground that would begin
to whip like a saw blade.
at times he looked down

and saw his hands were sticks,
his thighs hairy as a coyote's

on Saturday nights no reason
to go to town

to bed early the horses came up
snorting and chomping around in the dark.

alone in the empty bunkhouse
he slept one arm thrown out the window.

Sins of the Tongue

The tongue is a bit between the teeth
that the whole body follows.
when you speak a mist shoots
droplets before you, rainbows, clouds,
a burning pillar swerving over the plain
that beckons and calls you on and on.
in day and night dreams
a phantasmagoria with legs and fingers
that looms toward the face,
a passing rain
sprinkling the tongue and ears. . . .

or to keep it folded
into the wet parts of the mouth,
a snake swirling in a barrel,
a snake finding a place among leaves;
you go straight as a ship bulldozing
over the land with the rudder jammed;
the jaws curl around it.
afternoons the skin and teeth overheat
and the nights praise you with auroras;
you grow brittle. . . .

until it shoots from the head
                    all muscle,
until like the swelling Phoenix
you stand skin clothed in flame and words,
eyes empty.

Poem

I

There are no medals for loneliness.
above us the sky thickens toward poison,
a curdling sperm flow with thin lines, parts
of swimming figures, an arm
a leg, a face torn into the shape
of horror. a radiant
mother arched to feed
on her emerging children.
and though we have passed through cities,
struck deep into the reserves,
corpses line the path dropped
from the tide gone before.
and at night see all around us the wire parabolas
shifting into spirals that intersect and send out others.
by morning a road chews through the calf
and we black out into the sound of a stone crusher.

II

Now I know what it means to say farewell forever.
at sunset the lions snaking through the cold trees.
the bears bristling,
a wind in the blood.
the windows of my shoes open into the earth.

at the end of this life
there is no other.
I sleep with one hand
            thrown out of bed
gripping a knife
to guard my heart,

a black tongue
in a little cardboard box.
once filled with light
the eyes sink into the head toward a pool of ether
through the pinpoints of nerves.
there are no medals for this loneliness.
and the hand swollen beyond its shape
slowly turns, searching for a root and a throat.

The Farmer from Iowa

When the first taint of blue is on the fox's mouth
they are down here with their frozen breads
and peach preserves, in a moment driving
straight through in the old spongy Chrysler.

she stands on the front porch
waving letters beneath the winter
that passes over us, snow that
fills the granite crevices of heaven, watery skins
showing urine in their thin veins.
from each a cold puffs out.

and while the bishops doze
in their chasubles, beneath their heavy hats,
and their tiny wasted children kneel asleep
he is out there waving the electric trimmer,
up on the roof, making smooth curves of the hedge,
out in the back yard at six o'clock
eyes closed breaking bottles.

flies back to have the cows polled.
remembers the horses in their stalls, the
great icy clouds. I go over
through the arbor to talk about
the Great War, as the flowers
hold out their white and gold funnels,
and the palms pass across our faces,
the shadows of snakes twisting in a coming sea.

Mantequilla de Cacahuate

When something clicks in her skull
like a duck's beak
there comes gliding down the road
through the tunnel to the morning
a ring of bone without marrow in it
clothed in a collar of fur, fast
as a man on a bicycle,
head bent made of iron

there a question flames in the lungs
flames shoot from her teeth. in the fields
the bulls just waking mount
each other and the sheep
standing awake all night
hocks rotting in the mud roll
in their green blood.

the cats stick like nuggets of gold
in the trees. as he passes wooden arm
outstretched hands her a letter
that means her salvation. later
eating the sacrifice flushed in
sweat, in the room
that doesn't know which way to turn, the bed
comes marching into the kitchen
presents itself a mouth open
and full of teeth for a second sleep.

The Poor

Nobody wants the poor.
the rich see them idle on street corners
and call the police, hold meetings, send
petitions to the mayor if they must have them,
preferring the old and the crippled.
even God doesn't want them.
what would He say, how would He
speak their language, dine with them? and assures
a large place far below
among golden heaps of bones where they spend ages
carving goat horns, a reservoir
for the disturbed, the politically frustrated—where
for generations they wax unmolested
in their rags, carving their fantastic
saints, with swollen, fruit-like
teats, archaic smiles,
and a variety of curious sins.

The Harp and the Goat

The giant drums his thick fingers
half asleep in his cups, and the thunder
rolls over the rough oak boards, like the goat on his heap
wagging his tail and making the hairs, the rain
fall—floods over the giant crenels and beyond

to where the princess on her manure pile
primps, fish muscles aglow, hearing it
a call to the arms of her womanhood floating like a smoke
across her mirror. while below a machine
churns in her bowels as if eating men
and rising through her sinuses the steam
drives her mad making images.

oh Jack with the golden harp
you stroke the fishes out of the
grey sea that rise to your bidding and recite
the verses on their ash skins—the brown natives
run out tearing themselves to catch it in their paper cups—but
a rainbow by the tail dissolving and dissolving
as you play, as you must play, calling the cows out
from their mountain boulders that
know all, and heads lowered feed on your bowels.

The Fat Lady

Babies aren't usually
born that way.
ballooned in her orange
shift and hurled through
the safety glass plate
still clutching her ice-cream cone,
doubled up screaming through the air
so that somewhere she caught and
her belly opened to let out the gasp,
closed again fold over fold on itself;
astounded in her red smiles she lay
weeping, though dead.
and it wasn't till later they found
a cheek married to the ditch grass and mud, not
knowing what it is, blue
and starting to sputter, a leather cannonball
blasted through a brick wall
still clutched by the cord, a fuse
that came out as a tail, but
unscratched. marked for life, reading
about it, my wife said he
had been meant to live.

The Fat Lady

Cochise

You are the last person in the world I want to see today
yet you sit in my leather chair
I put my arm around you, light your cigar
and get out my best liquor,
even find in the refrigerator
miraculously some canapés. from this distance
your face curls through the smoke.
I am a traveller on shipboard seeing
the sun rising through mists in the wrong place.
troubles with family, friends, and church,
hear about your one-legged lover,
that he had nothing else but love to give.
you want to know how I do it, keeping sane.
but experienced I know what to say,
giving courage, while your breasts slump beneath the sweater,
the nipples looking around my room like baby birds
expecting food. they start to eye me. they want
to bite me on the face. but I
am drifting backwards in my dentist's chair,
on the trail with the lion
and Cochise, our stronghold, his
heart in his teeth, taking strength from the beast.
flattened by the weight of hot stones
I labored up with in my pack, my hands
veins climbing over the labyrinth,
to be lost now watching him, slipping out
to give it a try. he shows me how. we win. . . .
but you are so far out on the flats,
a mud woman rearing from the landscape,
dissolving in her own salt lake.
the person we fear most, a boy
driving his sheep across the sky with a stick—
they stumble, sparks fly from their hooves, their curly heads.

you scream as the stars dive down
to eat your hair. powdered gold coats my lips.
and he smiling opens his pouch,
takes my arm. we begin to dance,
and though I wait for you
he knows about the promises, the exchange—
we swear never to go back.

Dog Hospital

Riding by there every day
surrounded by eucalyptuses and palms
I hear them barking behind the whitewashed adobe fence,
see from my bicycle the ladies going in carrying
the loved ones in their arms—
in fact have been there myself
met the receptionist smiling beneath her cap,
read the magazines on training waiting
for the nodding Japanese man
who tries to pet her as he gives her shots,
gets bitten on the hand. nevertheless
days later she comes out smiling, refreshed
as she jumps into my arms and he almost
bowing winks. though riding by now
there are stories of those others calling
over the walls, that they are left to starve,
given other brains, arms
sewn to their necks, and
some are locked in cannisters,
lowered down polished tubes
into caves where there is no light
except the candle in their heads,
and the shadows around them that they
seeing now bark at.

Salvation

Because of the weather
the firetrucks have gone screaming in battalions
up the slick freeways, through the blinking lights
into the east, golden jaws set, their long
skeletons rattling behind.
cowboys have been reported
massing, growing fur like spores in the next valley.
the sky grows dark—edging over the mountains,
great worms at 3 o'clock, exactly as the stations
                              up the line informed us.
the Red Cross is handing out cards in the cathedral,
your skin is a tearing wet leather.
immediately the sheriff and his deputies have been dismissed
on charges of love of guilt, and sent to Florida
in retirement. the two buses and their snow plow
safe with bouquets and the tears of brides
nose up Mt. Lemmon to rescue
the girlscouts. they come down cheering
and in time for a slumber party.
while others left behind absolutely still, listen
to the music of the snow, their hands turn perfume,
waiting for the doors of their shacks to shatter open.
a plane with its tourists has gone down
over the Grand Canyon. miles away
searchers have begun striking out.
but still whole it keeps going down, down. . . .
between the cracks yellow arms
        reach in and around their throats.

Juan Sin Miedo

If he should hear above him
       a voice calling, saying
     Shall I fall, or shall I not
it will be all the same to him
       and throws the skeleton into the corner.
at night all the toilets begin to flush
      the cupboards swing open
   and scratching he goes across the pitching floor
  to join the mourners, smokes,
      tosses his butt after theirs into the dead man's mouth.
and meeting the owner on the road
    puts his clothes on as he takes them off,
                 says good-bye
       and departs like an arrow straight to heaven.
all these cows and barns that at night
          glow like frost,
    the furniture that talks
   and the mills by day that grind on and on. . . .
he walks among his enchanted corn
     sees the mountains race around like lions,
   strolls through the village then
  back to read a magazine, unwrap an old cigar,
waiting feet up for the knock
    of the governor stooped before the door
          with his daughter behind,
  who in time will come
or perhaps not.

The Night-Blooming Cereus

Cowboys and Indians
found them by smelling around at night,
because they grew deep in thickets

ate the moon of a tuber,
like eating their own souls.

our next-door neighbor,
who we hardly know,
comes knocking late
         and we go fumbling
over stones, around her husband's old paintings
to see it detached from its rotting broom pole,
floating in the flashlight around the garden

spend the rest of the night
barefoot on the warm patio
         telling jokes
      drinking their good whiskey.

my whole life is a trance
I hope to break from
      once or twice a year.

Phelps-Dodge

I

I want to tell you I am unlike the trees
in the rain the oily sheep gather around me
                                        like envelopes,
wearing the egg-stained canvas pants of a sailor

the same that shoot underground
and funnel through the walls of buildings
to appear like sparks,
baked potatoes burst from heat
from the ears of secretaries

delighted they go home
down through the clouds, more skinny,
a tongue, a chalk beak sticking out as a breastbone,
stepping over our reflections in puddles.

II

the trees are made of glass.
as we go through them they shatter
and mend like icicles
making a child's music.
as we touch them a fur
comes off on our hands.

Sun Tea

Across the street the neighbor
      in his shorts
looking like a thin Ernest Hemingway
is loading his panel truck
        with wicker baskets
to take on his vacation to Montana
           to paint clouds

while his daughter
nalga rich
behind the grove of tamarisks
runs around the house at midnight
        screaming in her swimsuit
      with all the lights on.

blood drips from the faucet.
my lids are enflamed
    like the corona of a sun
      that has long gone down.

the heat is pouring up from the
        hard calcareous ground;
the clouds float like heavy ink spots
      above the piny Catalinas.

27

DATE DUE